G000241110

Master Maths at Home

Numbers to 10

Scan the QR code to help your child's learning at home.

 | **MATHS**
NO PROBLEM!

mastermathsathome.com

How to use this book

Maths — No Problem! created **Master Maths at Home** to help children develop fluency in the subject and a rich understanding of core concepts.

Key features of the Master Maths at Home books include:

- Carefully designed lessons that provide structure but also allow flexibility in how they're used. For example, some children may want to write numbers, while others might want to trace.

- Speech bubbles containing content designed to spark diverse conversations, with many discussion points that don't have obvious 'right' or 'wrong' answers.

- Rich illustrations that will guide children to a discussion of shapes and units of measurement, allowing them to make connections to the wider world around them.

- Exercises that allow a flexible approach and can be adapted to suit any child's cognitive or functional ability.

- Clearly laid out pages that encourage children to practise a range of higher-order skills.

- A community of friendly and relatable characters who introduce each lesson and come along as your child progresses through the series.

You can see more guidance on how to use these books at **mastermathsathome.com**.

We're excited to share all the ways you can learn maths!

Copyright © 2022 Maths — No Problem!

Maths — No Problem!
mastermathsathome.com
www.mathsnoproblem.com
hello@mathsnoproblem.com

First published in Great Britain in 2022 by
Dorling Kindersley Limited
One Embassy Gardens, 8 Viaduct Gardens, London SW11 7BW
A Penguin Random House Company

The authorised representative in the EEA is Dorling Kindersley
Verlag GmbH. Arnulfstr. 124, 80636 Munich, Germany

10 9 8 7 6 5 4 3 2 1
001–327062–Jan/22

A CIP catalogue record for this book is available from the British Library.

ISBN: 978-0-24153-890-6
Printed and bound in China

For the curious
www.dk.com

This book was made with Forest Stewardship Council™ certified paper - one small step in DK's commitment to a sustainable future. For more information go to www.dk.com/our-green-pledge

Acknowledgements
The publisher would like to thank the authors and consultants Andy Psarianos, Judy Hornigold, Adam Gifford and Dr Anne Hermanson.

The Castledown typeface has been used with permission from the Colophon Foundry.

Contents

Ruby   Elliott   Amira   Charles   Lulu   Sam   Oak   Holly   Ravi   Emma   Jacob   Hannah

Counting to 10

Starter

Write the missing numbers.

1, 2, 3, ☐ , 5, 6, ☐ , 8, 9, 10

Can you help Ruby by writing the missing numbers?

Example

I can count to 10.
1, 2, 3, 4, 5, 6, 7, 8, 9, 10

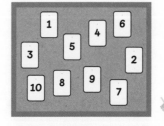

I can use the numbers on the wall.

Practice

Count and fill in the blanks.

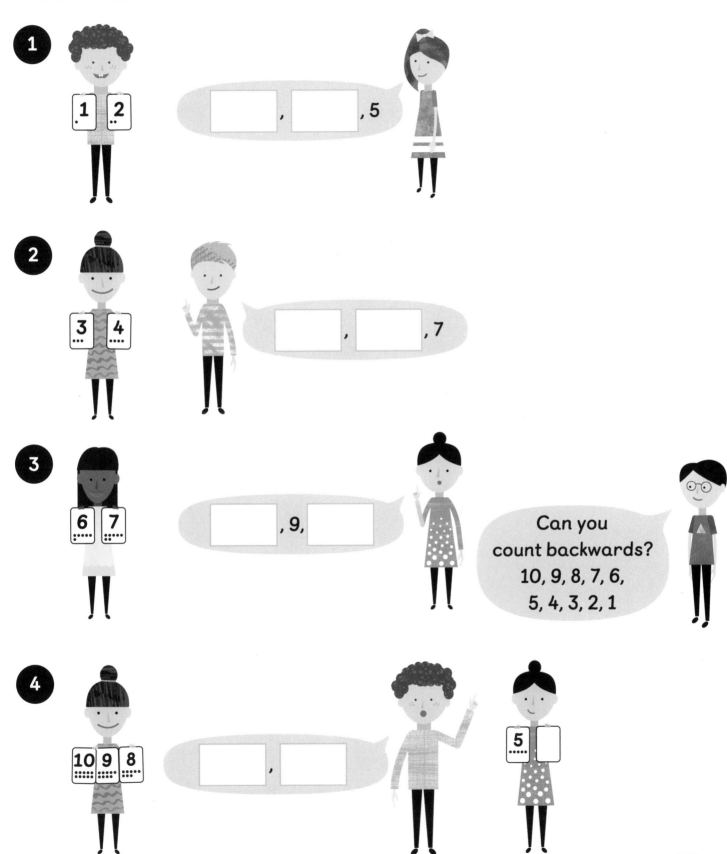

1. **1** **2** [ ], [ ], 5

2. **3** **4** [ ], [ ], 7

3. **6** **7** [ ], 9, [ ]

   Can you count backwards?
   10, 9, 8, 7, 6, 5, 4, 3, 2, 1

4. **10** **9** **8** [ ], [ ] **5**

Counting things

How many carrots is Hannah washing?

Example

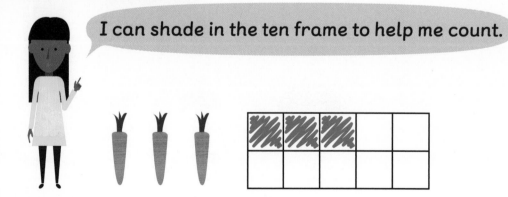

I can shade in the ten frame to help me count.

Hannah is washing 3 carrots.

Practice

Count and shade 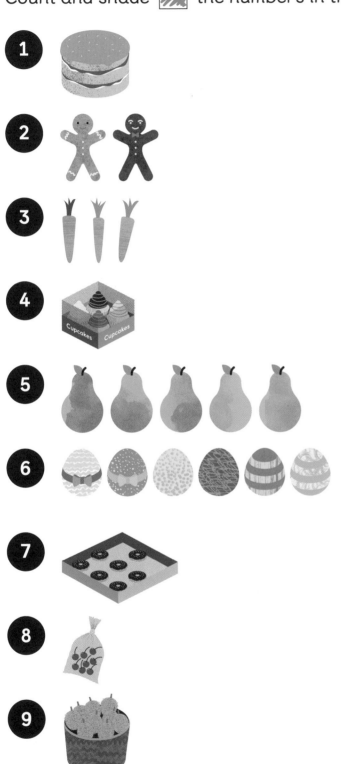 the numbers in the ☐☐☐☐☐ .

		1 one
1	🍔	
2	🍪🍪	2 two
3	🥕🥕🥕	3 three
4	🧁	4 four
5	🍐🍐🍐🍐🍐	5 five
6	🥚🥚🥚🥚🥚🥚	6 six
7	🍩	7 seven
8	🍒	8 eight
9	🍓	9 nine
10	🍪	10 ten

Reading and writing to 10

Starter

How many teddy bears are there?

Example

I can shade in the ten frame to help me count.

5
five

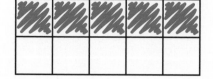

I followed the dots with my pen to write the number and the word.

There are 5 teddy bears.

1 Count and shade, and then trace the numbers.

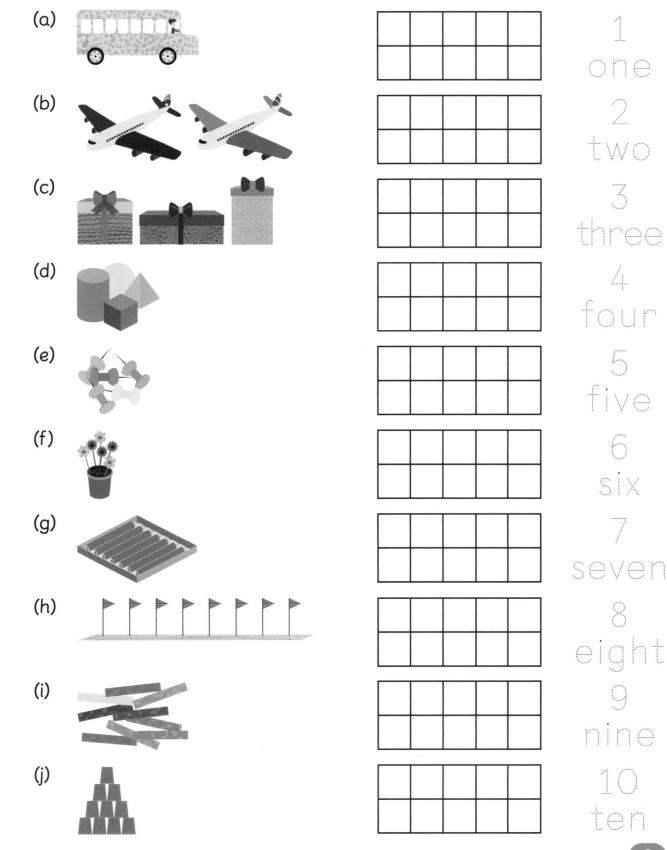

(a)

1
one

(b)

2
two

(c)

3
three

(d)

4
four

(e)

5
five

(f)

6
six

(g)

7
seven

(h)

8
eight

(i)

9
nine

(j)

10
ten

2 Trace and match.

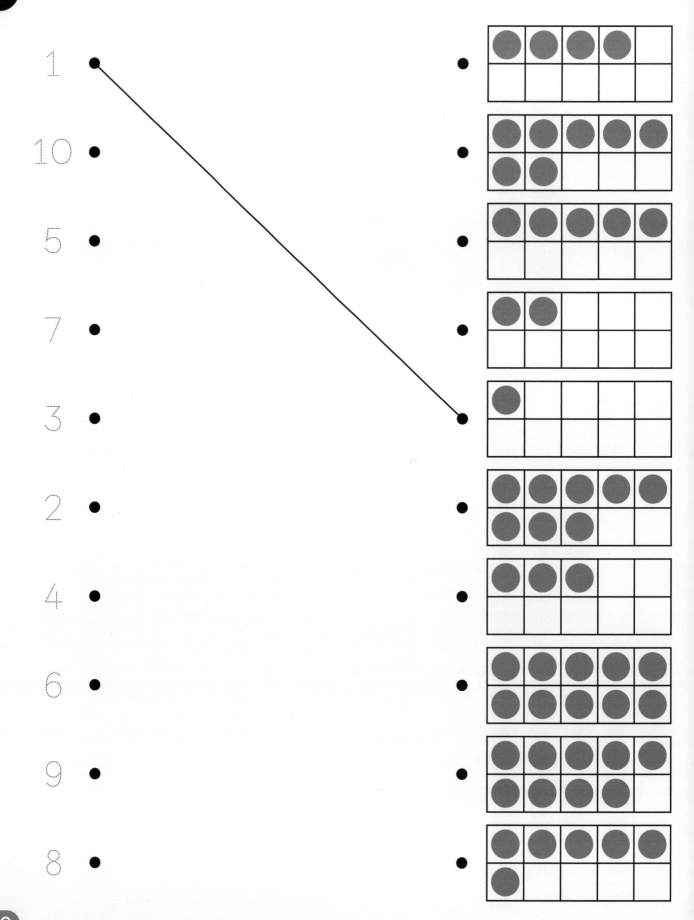

1

10

5

7

3

2

4

6

9

8

3 Trace and match.

one •

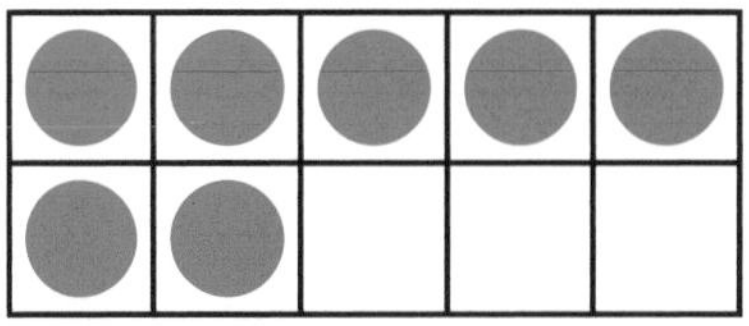

four •

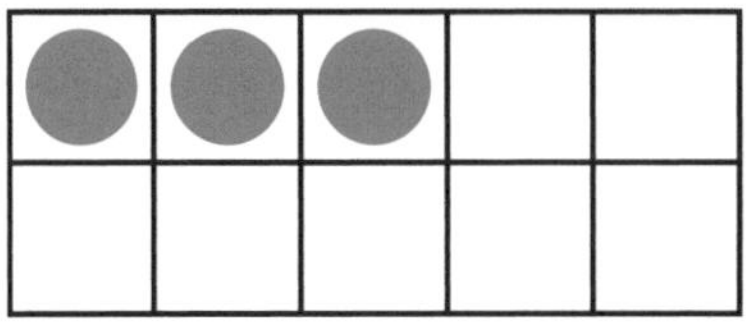

nine •

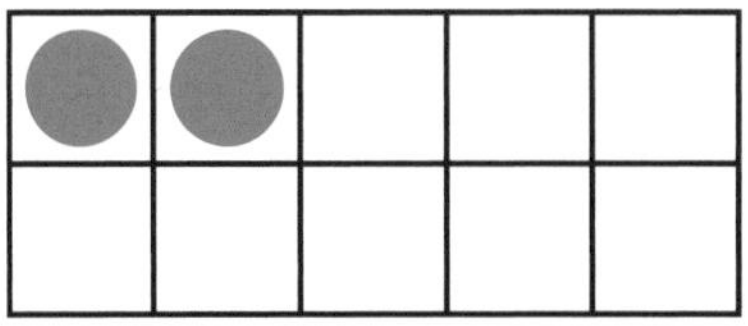

ten •

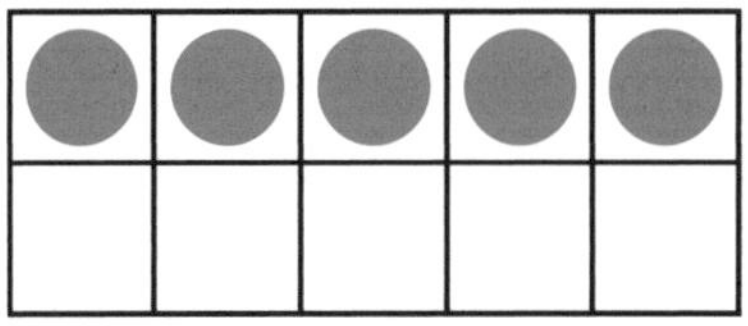

six •

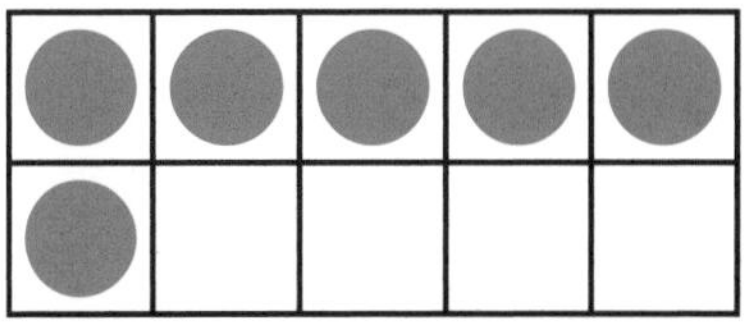

three •

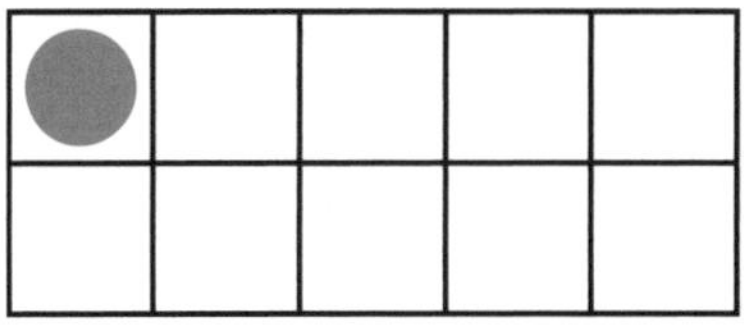

seven •

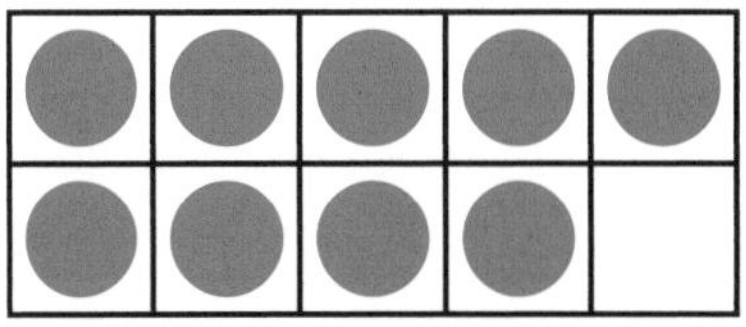

two •

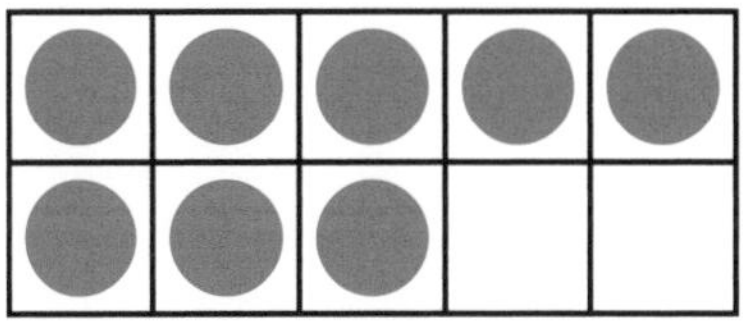

five •

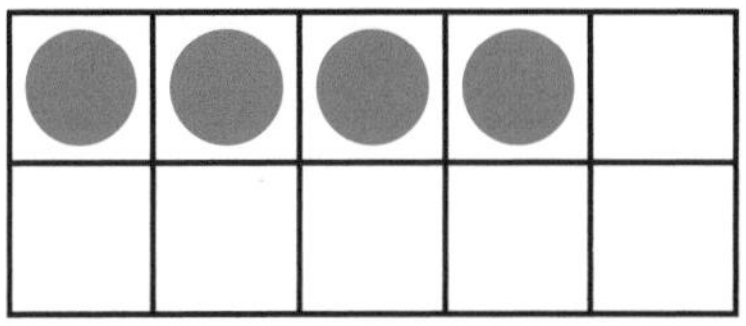

eight •

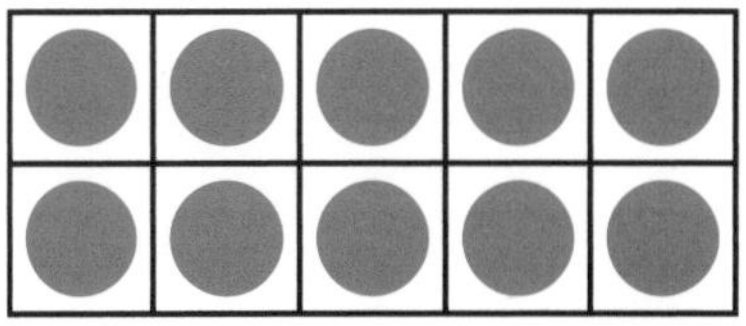

Comparing and ordering numbers

Starter

Are there enough bananas and apples for everyone?

Example

1

I can line them up to check.

 4 bananas

I can use cubes to check.

  5 children

  7 apples

There are more apples than children.

There are fewer bananas than children.

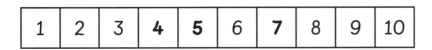

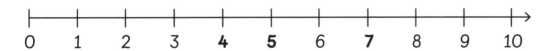

There are 4 . There are 5 .

4 is less than 5.

There are not enough  for each 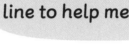 .

There are 7 . There are 5 .

7 is more than 5.

There are enough for each .

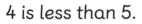

I can use a number line to help me as well.

2 3

6

8

Which number is the greatest?
Which number is the smallest?

8 is more than 3.
8 is more than 6.
8 is the **greatest** number.

3 is less than 8.
3 is less than 6.
3 is the **smallest** number.

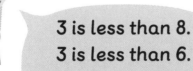

1 Count. Circle the group that has more and fill in the blanks.

(a) [ ] is less than [ ] .

(b)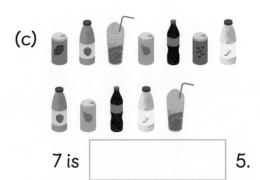

[ ] is more than [ ] .

4 is 1 more than 3.
3 is 1 less than 4.

(c)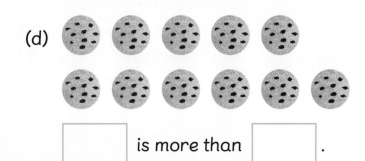

7 is [ ] 5.

(d)

[ ] is more than [ ] .

(e)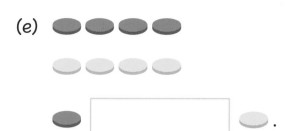

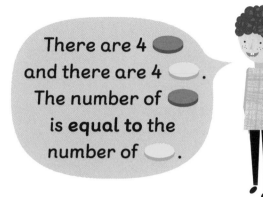
There are 4 🔴 and there are 4 ⚪. The number of 🔴 is **equal to** the number of ⚪.

2 Which number is smaller? Fill in the blanks.

(a)
| 4 | 5 | ☐ |

(b)
| 8 | 2 | ☐ |

(c)

(d)

(e)
| ⚫⚫⚫⚫ | 7 | ☐ |

(f)
| ⚫⚫⚫⚫⚫ | 6 | ☐ |

3 Which number is greater? Fill in the blanks.

(a)

| ••••• | **7** | |

(b)

| :•••• | **8** | |

(c)

| :•••• | •• | |

(d)

| •• | :•••• | |

(e)

| ••••• | **4** | |

(f)

| ::••• | **6** | |

4 Arrange the numbers in order from the smallest to the greatest.

| 1 | 2 | 3 | 4 | 5 | 6 | 7 | 8 | 9 | 10 |

9   7   8

| | | |

smallest   ⟶   greatest

I can use the number track to help me.

5 Arrange the numbers in order from the greatest to the smallest.

2   4   3

[ ]   [ ]   [ ]

greatest   ——→   smallest

6 Fill in the blanks.

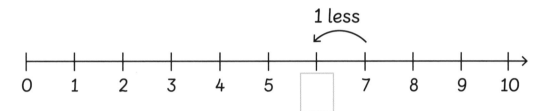

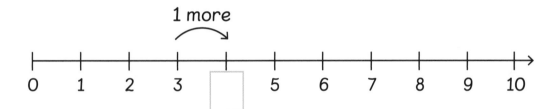

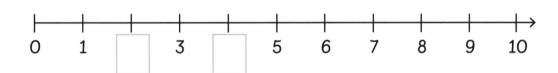

(a) [ ] is 1 less than 9.

(b) [ ] is 1 less than 6.

(c) [ ] is 1 more than 3.

(d) [ ] is 1 more than 6.

Number bonds

Starter

How many ways can you arrange the two-sided counters?

Example

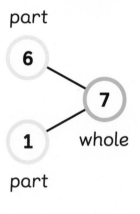

part

6

1

part

7

whole

This is called a number bond. It shows how a number can be split up into two numbers.

There are no yellow ⬭.
We can say there are 0 ⬭.
We can write 0 as zero.

I think that

7

7

0

makes 7 as well.

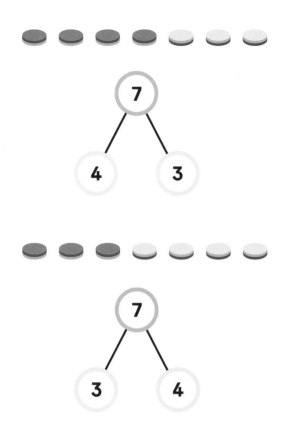

How many ways are there to make 7?

Practice

1 Fill in the blanks and complete the number bonds.

(a) [ ] and [ ] make 7.

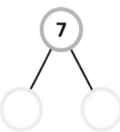

(b) [ ] and [ ] make 7.

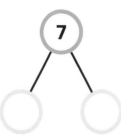

(c)

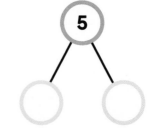

[ ] and [ ] make 5.

(d)

4 and 4 make [ ] .

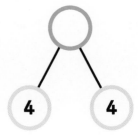

(e)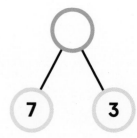

7 and 3 make [ ] .

(f)

2 and [ ] make 10.

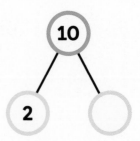

2 Write the answers and draw lines to match.

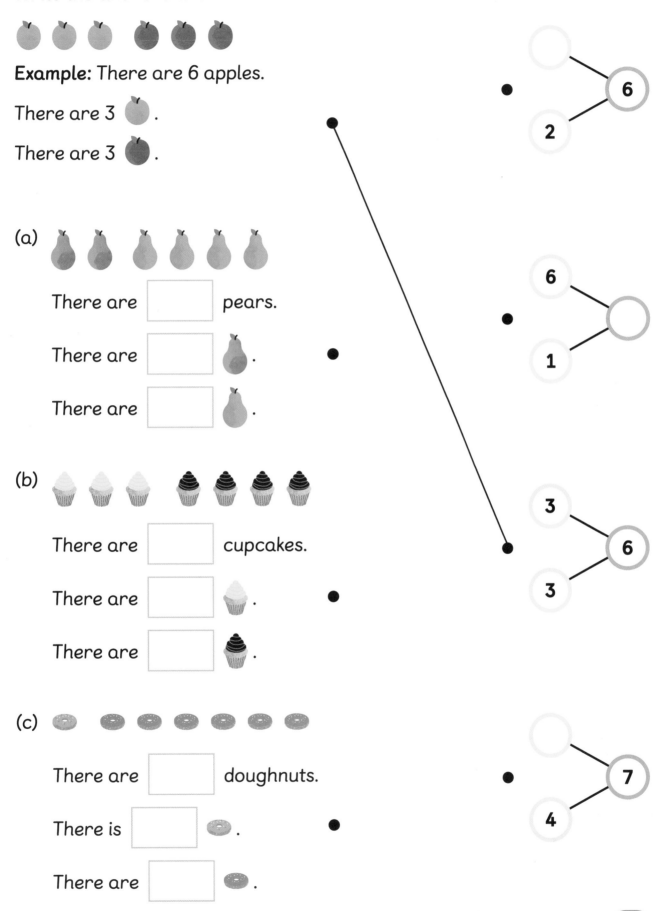

Example: There are 6 apples.

There are 3 🍎.

There are 3 🍎.

(a) There are ☐ pears.

There are ☐ 🍐.

There are ☐ 🍐.

(b) There are ☐ cupcakes.

There are ☐ 🧁.

There are ☐ 🧁.

(c) There are ☐ doughnuts.

There is ☐ 🍩.

There are ☐ 🍩.

Adding with number bonds

Starter

How many birds are there in total?

Example

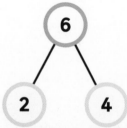

We can also write 2 + 4 = 6.

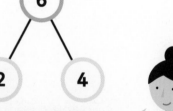

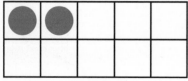

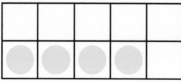

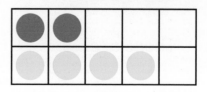

2   +   4   =   6

There are 6 birds in total.

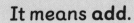

This is a plus sign.

It means **add**.

$2 + 4 = 6$

This is an **equals sign**.

$2 + 4 = 6$ is an addition equation.

We say two plus four equals six.

Practice

1. Fill in the blanks and complete the number bonds.

   (a)

   There are ⬜ .

   There are ⬜ .

   There are ⬜ hats in total.

   ⬜ + ⬜ = ⬜

(b)

There are ⬚ .

There are ⬚ .

There are ⬚ bags altogether.

⬚ + ⬚ = ⬚

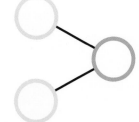

(c)

There are ⬚ .

There are ⬚   .

There are ⬚ purses altogether.

⬚ + ⬚ = ⬚

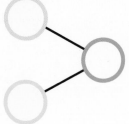

(d)

⬚ + ⬚ = ⬚

There are ⬚ in total.

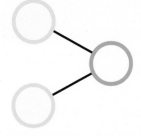

(e)

⬚ + ⬚ = ⬚

⬚ and ⬚ make ⬚ .

24

② Fill in the blanks and match.

(a)

$\boxed{}$ + $\boxed{}$ = $\boxed{}$

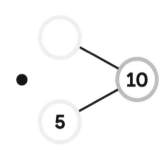

2
5
7

(b)

$\boxed{}$ + $\boxed{}$ = $\boxed{}$

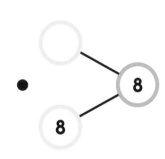

5
10

(c)
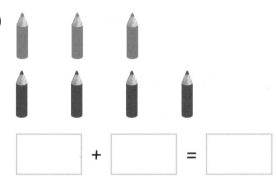

$\boxed{}$ + $\boxed{}$ = $\boxed{}$

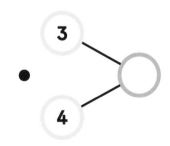

8
8

(d)

$\boxed{}$ + $\boxed{}$ = $\boxed{}$

3
4

(e)

$\boxed{}$ + $\boxed{}$ = $\boxed{}$

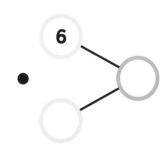

6

Adding by counting on

There are 6 snacks in the box.

How many snacks are there in total?

I know there are 6 snacks in the box. I don't need to count them.

1 6 + 3 = ?

Start from 6, then count 3 more.

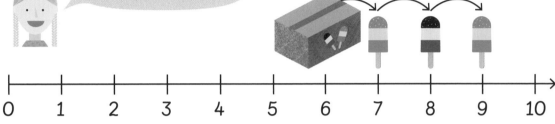

7, 8, 9

6 + 3 = 9

There are 9 snacks in total.

2 2 + 8 = ?

There are 8 bananas in the bunch. I can count on from 2.

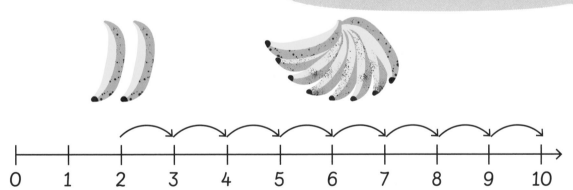

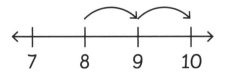

It's easier to count on like this.

2 + 8 = 10

There are 10 bananas altogether.

1 Count on to find the total number of objects.

(a)

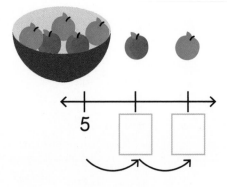

5 + 2 = ☐

There are ☐ apples in total.

(b)

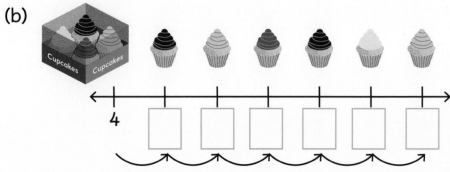

4 + 6 = ☐

There are ☐ cupcakes in total.

(c)

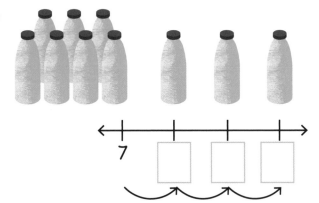

7 + 3 = ☐

There are ☐ drinks altogether.

2 Count on and fill in the blanks.

(a)

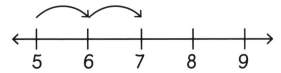

5 + 2 = ☐

(b)

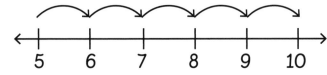

5 + ☐ = 10

(c)

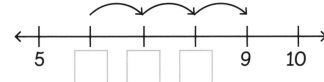

6 + 3 = ☐

Addition stories

What stories can you tell about what the children are wearing?

Example

We can tell number stories.

2 of the children have glasses on. 3 of the children do not have glasses on.

There are 5 children in total.

2   **+**   **3**   **=**   **5**

2 and 3 make 5.

5
2   3

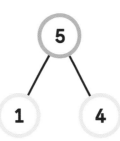

I can tell another story.
Only 1 child has a hat on.

There are 5 children.
1 child is wearing a hat.
4 children are not wearing hats.

5 = 1 + 4

5
1   4

5 is 1 and 4.

3 of the children are dressed in blue.

3 of the children are wearing blue.
2 of the children are wearing yellow.

3 + 2 = 5

5
3   2

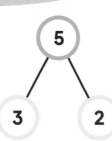

3 and 2 make 5.

1 Fill in the blanks and complete the number bonds.

(a)

There are 8 frogs.

[   ] frogs are sitting.

[   ] frogs are jumping.

[   ] + [   ] = 8

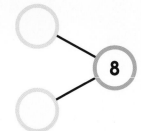

(b)

There are [   ] in the pot.

There are [   ] in the pot.

There are [   ] flowers in total.

2 Look at the picture and fill in the blanks.

(a) There are [ ] bears in total.

There are [ ] black bears.

There are [ ] brown bears.

[ ] + [ ] = 10

(b) There are [ ] bear cubs.

There are [ ] adult bears.

[ ] + [ ] = [ ]

Young bears are called bear cubs.

Can you make other number stories from the picture?

Subtract by crossing out

Starter

There were 9 oranges on the tree.

4 oranges fell to the ground.

How many oranges are left on the tree?

Example

9 – 4 = 5

There are 5 oranges left on the tree.

I can cross out 4 oranges to show the oranges that fell off the tree.

This is a **minus sign**.

It means **subtract**.

$$9 - 4 = 5$$

9 − 4 = 5 is a subtraction equation.

This is an **equals sign**.

We say nine minus four equals five.

Practice

Subtract by crossing out and then fill in the blanks.

1

7 − ☐ = ☐

2

7 − ☐ = ☐

3

☐ − 1 = ☐

Subtract by using number bonds

Starter

How many hippos are not muddy?

Example

We can subtract to find how many hippos are not muddy.

There are 7 hippos in total.
4 hippos are muddy.

7 - 4 = 3

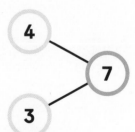

3 hippos are not muddy.

Complete the number bonds and fill in the blanks.

1 How many mice are not ?

There are 8 mice.

6 are .

8 – 6 = [ ]

There are [ ] .

[ ] mice are not .

2

How many doughnuts are not ?

There are 5 doughnuts.

There are [ ] .

5 – [ ] = [ ]

There are [ ] .

[ ] doughnuts are not .

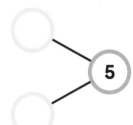

Subtract by counting back

Starter

I started with 10 pastries. I put some of them in the box.

How many pastries are in the box?

Example

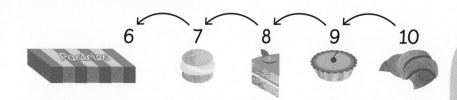

The baker started with 10 pastries. I can count back 4 from 10 to subtract.

10 – 4 = 6

There are 6 pastries in the box.

I can use a number track to help me count back.

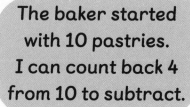

| 1 | 2 | 3 | 4 | 5 | 6 | 7 | 8 | 9 | 10 |

1 Subtract by counting back. Fill in the blanks.

There are 8 toys in total.
How many toys are in the box?

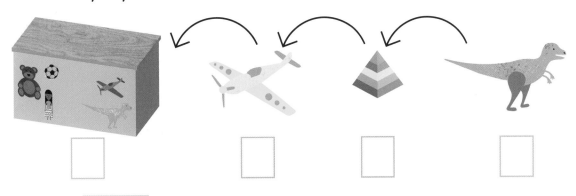

8 – 3 =

2 Use the number track to help you count back.

(a) 9 – 5 =

| 1 | 2 | 3 | 4 | 5 | 6 | 7 | 8 | 9 | 10 |

(b) 5 – 2 =

| 1 | 2 | 3 | 4 | 5 | 6 | 7 | 8 | 9 | 10 |

(c) 7 – 4 =

| 1 | 2 | 3 | 4 | 5 | 6 | 7 | 8 | 9 | 10 |

(d) 6 – 5 =

| 1 | 2 | 3 | 4 | 5 | 6 | 7 | 8 | 9 | 10 |

Subtraction stories

Can you tell a subtraction story using this picture?

Example

I can tell a subtraction story. There were 6 monkeys in the tree, but 2 jumped off.
6 − 2 = 4
There are 4 monkeys left in the tree.

I can tell a different subtraction story.

There are 6 monkeys.
5 of the monkeys are brown.
6 − 5 = 1
1 of the monkeys is
not brown.

Practice

Fill in the blanks and complete the number bonds.

1

There are ☐ kittens.

☐ kittens are sleeping.

The rest are sitting.

9 − 4 = ☐

☐ kittens are sitting.

4

2 There are ☐ kittens.

☐ kittens are .

The rest of the kittens are .

☐ − ☐ = ☐

☐ are .

Review and challenge

1 Fill in the blanks.

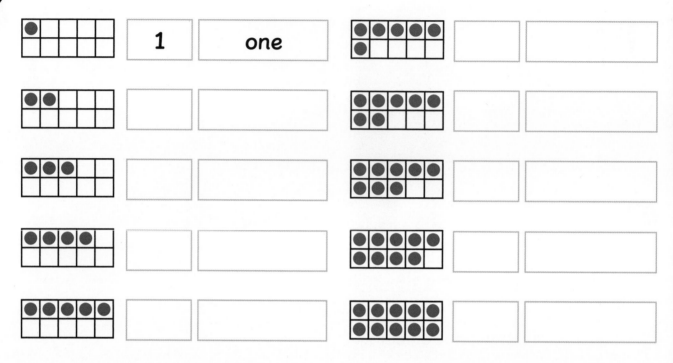

(a) Arrange from the smallest to the greatest.

(i)   5   10   8

smallest ⟶ greatest

(ii)   4   5   2

smallest ⟶ greatest

(b) Arrange from the greatest to the smallest.

(i)   6   5   8

greatest ⟶ smallest

(ii)   2   7   1

greatest ⟶ smallest

(c) Fill in the blanks.

[ ] is 1 more than 8.   [ ] is 1 less than 7.

(d) There are 8 bananas altogether.
Some are already in the bag.

[ ] bananas will be added to the bag.

[ ] + [ ] = [ ]

---

2 Fill in the blanks.

(a)

1	2	3	4	5	6	7	8	9	10

7 − 3 = [ ]

(b)

1	2	3	4	5	6	7	8	9	10

10 − 2 = [ ]

(c)

[ ] school chairs   [ ] school chairs

[ ] + [ ] = [ ] school chairs

3 Fill in the blanks and match.

(a) $7 - 5 =$ ☐ ●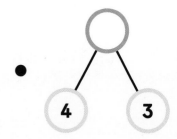

(b) $4 + 3 =$ ☐ ●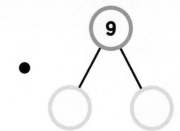

(c) ☐ $= 2 + 4$ ●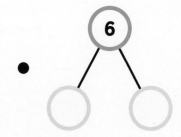

(d) $9 - 6 =$ ☐ ●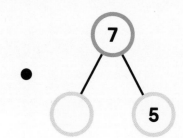

4

Look at the picture, fill in the blanks and complete the number bonds.

(a) ☐ are on the sand.

☐  are not on the sand.

☐ + ☐ = ☐

There are ☐ in total.

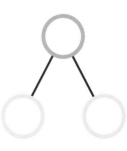

(b) There are ☐ children at the beach.

☐ of the children are playing in the water.

☐ − ☐ = ☐

☐ children are not playing in the water.

Answers

Page 5 **1** 3, 4 **2** 5, 6 **3** 8, 10 **4** 7, 6, 4.

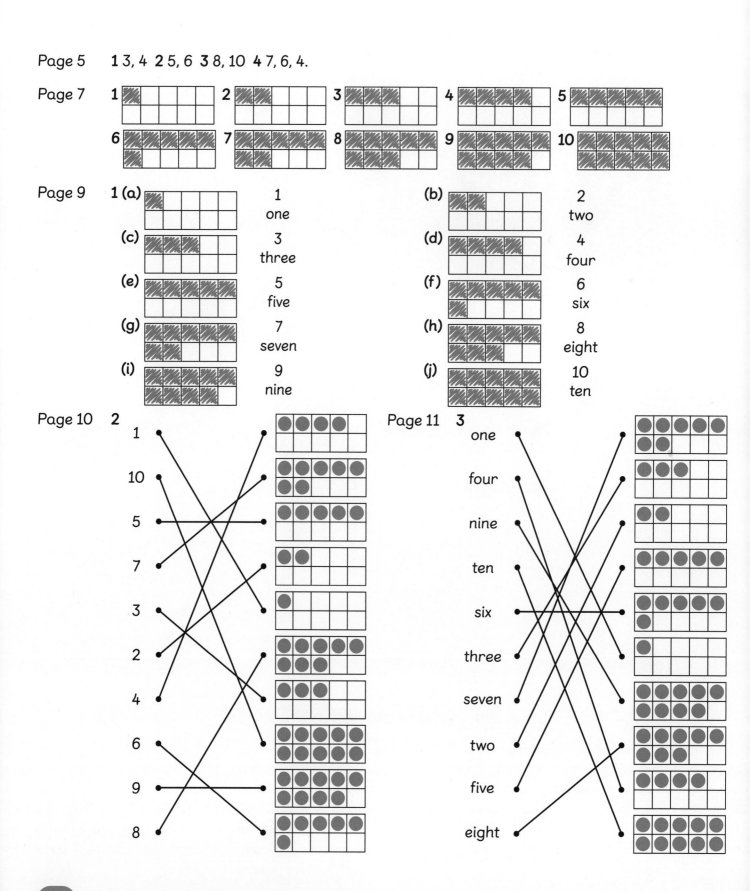

Page 14   **1 (a)** 3, 6 **(b)** 4, 3 **(c)** more than **(d)** 6, 5.

Page 15   **(e)** is equal to. **2 (a)** 4 **(b)** 2 **(c)** 5 **(d)** 1 **(e)** 4 **(f)** 6.

Page 16   **3 (a)** 7 **(b)** 8 **(c)** 6 **(d)** 6 **(e)** 5 **(f)** 7 **4** 7, 8, 9.

Page 17   **5** 4, 3, 2 **6 (a)** 8 **(b)** 5 **(c)** 4 **(d)** 7.

Page 19   **1** Possible answers: 3 and 4, 2 and 5, 1 and 6 and 0 and 7.

Page 20   **(c)** 3 and 2 make 5 **(d)** 4 and 4 make 8 **(e)** 7 and 3 make 10 **(f)** 2 and 8 make 10.

Page 21   **2**

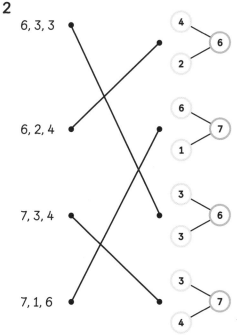

Page 23   **1 (a)** There are 4 green hats. There are 3 red hats. There are 7 hats in total. 4 + 3 = 7.

Page 24   **(b)** There are 2 kit bags. There are 3 shoulder bags. There are 5 bags altogether. 2 + 3 = 5 **(c)** There are 6 red purses. There are 2 purple purses. There are 8 purses altogether. 6 + 2 = 8 **(d)** 4 + 0 = 4. There are 4 cupcakes in total. **(e)** 6 + 4 = 10. 6 and 4 make 10.

Page 25   **2**

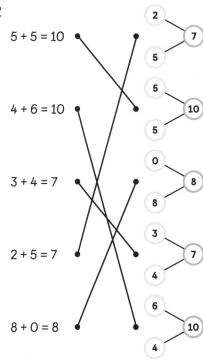

Page 28   **1 (a)** 5 + 2 = 7. There are 7 apples in total. **(b)** There are 10 cupcakes in total. 4 + 6 = 10.

Page 29   **(c)** 7 + 3 = 10. There are 10 drinks altogether. **2 (a)** 5 + 2 = 7 **(b)** 5 + 5 = 10 **(c)** 6 + 3 = 9

Page 32   **1 (a)** 6 frogs are sitting. 2 frogs are jumping. 6 + 2 = 8 **(b)** There are 4 pink flowers. There are 3 yellow flowers. There are 7 flowers altogether.

Page 33   **2 (a)** There are 10 bears in total. There are 3 black bears. There are 7 brown bears. 3 + 7 = 10 **(b)** There are 4 bear cubs. There are 6 adult bears. 4 + 6 = 10.

Page 35   **1** 7 − 5 = 2 **2** 7 − 0 = 7 **3** 6 − 1 = 5.

Page 37   **1** 2. There are 2 white mice. 2 mice are not brown. **2** There are 2 pink doughnuts. 5 − 2 = 3. There are 3 blue doughnuts. 3 doughnuts are not pink.

Answers continued

Page 39   **1** 5, 6, 7, 8   8 − 3 = 5   **2 (a)** 9 − 5 = 4
(b) 5 − 2 = 3   **(c)** 7 − 4 = 3   **(d)** 6 − 5 = 1

Page 41   **1** There are 9 kittens. 4 kittens are sleeping. 9 − 4 = 5. 5 kittens are sitting. **2** There are 9 kittens. 6 kittens are grey. 9 − 6 = 3. 3 kittens are brown.

Page 42   **1 (a)** 5, 8, 10. 2, 4, 5 **(b)** 8, 6, 5. 7, 2, 1.

Page 43   **(c)** 9 is 1 more than 8. 6 is one less than 7. **(d)** 3 bananas will be added to the bag. 5 + 3 = 8 **2 (a)** 7 − 3 = 4 **(b)** 10 − 2 = 8 **(c)** 0 school chairs + 9 school chairs = 9 school chairs.

Page 44   **3 (a)**   **(b)**

(c)   **(d)**

Page 45   **4 (a)** 4 puffins are on the sand. 2 puffins are not on the sand. 4 + 2 = 6 **(b)** There are 4 children playing at the beach. 2 children are in the water. 4 − 2 = 2. 2 children are not in the water.